INSPIRATIONAL HASHTAGS

100 Tweetable Moments That Speak To Your Inner Soul

#KimMM

KIM MILTON-MACKEY

ISBN: 1534992901
ISBN-13: 978-1534992900

Acknowledgments:

I desire to personally thank God for my life, health and strength, my immediate family for their contributions to my inspiration and knowledge and other help in creating this book; my lovely husband, Dexter Mackey, Jr., who has to listen to my unorthodox speeches daily; my beloved parents, Pastor Aaron & Virgie Milton, who embraced every crazy dream and gave me the fuel to see them through; my daughters, Jamie and Jameka, who stood by me through all my life-altering events; my other daughters, Nickeya, Charita, Mariah, TaShea, and Kierra, who endured my madness but yet believed in me and embraced me as their extended mother. I can't sign out until I pay homage to the entire Milton and Townsend Family who suffered greatly because of me being a nuisance. My life turned out to be great because of your support.

I acknowledge Nyshell Lawrence and Morgan M. Munlin for visualizing my business dreams; Melinda Dexter, my editor; and all my extended family members and friends which are too many to list. Everyone in my life is equally important and has played a crucial role in getting me to where I am today. I earnestly pray for each of you.

I love you all.

Introduction:

Inspiration is the process of being mentally stimulated to do or feel something, especially to do something creative. A **hashtag** is a type of label or metadata tag used on social networks which makes it easier for users to find messages with a specific theme or content.

Inspirational Hashtags is a collection of creative intuitive quotes that can be used universally via social media with minimal characters in mind. The inspirational declarations are meaningful and were downloaded in my spirit to share with the world.

This short-form book is filled with proverbs that came to me directly by way of revelatory delivery. Its content is filled with divine tweetable moments, timeless wisdom, and was inspired by the bible, various judicial speeches, political arguments, world events, and life experiences.

The book is designed to challenge your thinking patterns and encourages you to come up with various results that challenge your thought process. These hashtags can be used on all various social media outlets as retweets, posts, uploads, life lessons, or teachable moments.

After each hashtag#, you are encouraged to use your imagination and interpret the sayings in a way that resonates with your inner soul. You may find your responses helpful when later reflecting back to the book.

Now upload, post, and tweet away…

1.) Your aspirations, goals, dreams, and visions don't have expiration dates, but your lifespan does #KimMM

What is your interpretation of this statement?

_____

_____

_____

_____

2.) Technology removed the need for using our memory. We are literally crippled during a blackout #KimMM

What is your interpretation of this statement?

_____

_____

_____

_____

3.) **When you begin a new project, fear NOT. Just act like it's impossible to fail. Focus on strategies that increase your value #KimMM**

What is your interpretation of this statement?

_____

_____

_____

_____

4.) **If you see that the sky is clearly blue & hundreds see it as purple, don't change your view. Everybody can't see what you can see #KimMM**

What is your interpretation of this statement?

_____

_____

_____

_____

5.) **Open yourself up to people who accept that winning is not always the final result #KimMM**

What is your interpretation of this statement?

_____

_____

_____

_____

6.) **Our population is well acquainted with lack. Change is coming. Get positioned to embrace prosperity without sorrow #KimMM**

What is your interpretation of this statement?

_____

_____

_____

_____

7.) **Some may begin with ignorance, but humans were built with a genius gene that brings information to light #KimMM**

What is your interpretation of this statement?

_____

_____

_____

_____

8.) **Many were born with a diversity of gifts but few have the empowerment affect #KimMM**

What is your interpretation of this statement?

_____

_____

_____

_____

9.) It takes one voice to empower masses and invoke a radical movement #KimMM

What is your interpretation of this statement?

_____

_____

_____

_____

10.) The power of collaboration can be the missing piece to your puzzle. The one man/woman show is over #KimMM

What is your interpretation of this statement?

_____

_____

_____

_____

11.) **When some races carry weapons, it's a right, but when others carry it, then it's a threat #KimMM**

What is your interpretation of this statement?

_____

_____

_____

_____

12.) **Our faith teaches us the correct responses in ALL situations #KimMM**

What is your interpretation of this statement?

_____

_____

_____

_____

13.) Just because you have liberty to do it, doesn't mean it's ethical to do #KimMM

What is your interpretation of this statement?

_____

_____

_____

_____

14.) Be careful who gives you direction when you are lost on the highway of life. Seeking one with travel experience may offer a shortcut #KimMM

What is your interpretation of this statement?

_____

_____

_____

_____

15.) There comes a time in your life where you have to make "Destiny Decisions" #KimMM

What is your interpretation of this statement?

_____

_____

_____

_____

16.) A hostage mentality is built with fear #KimMM

What is your interpretation of this statement?

_____

_____

_____

_____

17.) When human behavior looks too close to a deadly weapon, take cover #KimMM

What is your interpretation of this statement?

_____

_____

_____

_____

18.) Be careful of mentors that have a pure motive to manipulate #KimMM

What is your interpretation of this statement?

_____

_____

_____

_____

19.) Chastisement is the sister to development #KimMM

What is your interpretation of this statement?

_____

_____

_____

_____

20.) Does your cause start fires or fuel fires? there is a difference in the outcome #KimMM

What is your interpretation of this statement?

_____

_____

_____

_____

21.) Faith citizens dare not be an embarrassment to the Ecclesia body #KimMM

What is your interpretation of this statement?

_____

_____

_____

_____

22.) Leaders must remember when you have no more patience to give to those following you, it's time to relinquish your authority #KimMM

What is your interpretation of this statement?

_____

_____

_____

_____

23.) Flint Water Crisis Disaster relief money given to the OPPRESSOR to allocate & distribute fairly. SMH, this is Government madness #KimMM

What is your interpretation of this statement?

_____

_____

_____

_____

24.) When a final choice is made, own it, don't hide when matters crumble. Be prepared to live out the results from your decision #KimMM

What is your interpretation of this statement?

_____

_____

_____

_____

25.) **Existing & soon-to-be leaders, certain mistakes or errors will warrant your demotion or dismissal. Be gracious in your departure #KimMM**

What is your interpretation of this statement?

_____

_____

_____

_____

26.) **The small but deadliest weapon in an election season is the pencil. There is no penalty to use it #KimMM**

What is your interpretation of this statement?

_____

_____

_____

_____

27.) **You get one railroad warning before a train wreck, heed the signal #KimMM**

What is your interpretation of this statement?

_____

_____

_____

_____

28.) **Stay the narrow course citizens of the Faith... greatness is ahead #KimMM**

What is your interpretation of this statement?

_____

_____

_____

_____

29.) Don't apologize for the things that are rightfully yours by design #KimMM

What is your interpretation of this statement?

_____

_____

_____

_____

30.) Regardless of status and position, you're not above questioning #KimMM

What is your interpretation of this statement?

_____

_____

_____

_____

31.) Minimize trial and error by asking first #KimMM

What is your interpretation of this statement?

_____

_____

_____

_____

32.) It may be your time, but not your turn. Stay in line. Your number will be called #KimMM

What is your interpretation of this statement?

_____

_____

_____

_____

33.) The struggle is oh so real, and so is the power of God #KimMM

What is your interpretation of this statement?

_____

_____

_____

_____

34.) Be relentless in your pursuit of destiny, but don't be afraid to slam on the brakes #KimMM

What is your interpretation of this statement?

_____

_____

_____

_____

35.) Nobody gave you your rank, you EARNED it #KimMM

What is your interpretation of this statement?

_____

_____

_____

_____

36.) Before you get in the game, take time to study your opponent's victory strategy #KimMM

What is your interpretation of this statement?

_____

_____

_____

_____

37.) **You were distinctly designed by our Creator, so stop apologizing for your uniqueness. Embrace the totality of YOU #KimMM**

What is your interpretation of this statement?

_____

_____

_____

_____

38.) **Pessimism removes the oxygen from the room. Pursue the air of optimism #KimMM**

What is your interpretation of this statement?

_____

_____

_____

_____

39.) Being nice doesn't require any skills, just acts of kindness #KimMM

What is your interpretation of this statement?

_____

_____

_____

_____

40.) It is evident when people don't have enough life experiences to see the importance of a suppressed record #KimMM

What is your interpretation of this statement?

_____

_____

_____

_____

41.) If love is to prevail, then Americans must REMOVE all labels when describing people and focus on human life #KimMM

What is your interpretation of this statement?

_____

_____

_____

_____

42.) You cannot make progress without making decisions #KimMM

What is your interpretation of this statement?

_____

_____

_____

_____

43.) Leaders who didn't master followership can become tyrants #KimMM

What is your interpretation of this statement?

_____

_____

_____

_____

44.) Making global spiritual impact via social media takes less time than witnessing #KimMM

What is your interpretation of this statement?

_____

_____

_____

_____

45.) Conflict is inevitable when TRUTH is absent #KimMM

What is your interpretation of this statement?

_____

_____

_____

_____

46.) When being politically and spiritually correct are looked down on, then pandemonium rules #KimMM

What is your interpretation of this statement?

_____

_____

_____

_____

47.) **When silence is my response, don't force me to verbally reply if you aren't prepared to hear my truth #KimMM**

What is your interpretation of this statement?

_____

_____

_____

_____

48.) **Knowledge and wisdom is bestowed upon us to create unique opportunities for those assigned to us #KimMM**

What is your interpretation of this statement?

_____

_____

_____

_____

49.) Your words carry power. Be known for creating an atmosphere of serenity #KimMM

What is your interpretation of this statement?

_____

_____

_____

_____

50.) When sensitive information is exposed, embrace for the storm of uncertainty #KimMM

What is your interpretation of this statement?

_____

_____

_____

_____

51.) A true heart repents prior to exposure #KimMM

What is your interpretation of this statement?

_____

_____

_____

_____

52.) It's undeniable when unity is present, there are no superstars #KimMM

What is your interpretation of this statement?

_____

_____

_____

_____

53.) Sometimes we protect what we value, even when it can destroy us #KimMM

What is your interpretation of this statement?

_____

_____

_____

_____

54.) Declaring peace in your atmosphere can give you the power to overcome chaos #KimMM

What is your interpretation of this statement?

_____

_____

_____

_____

55.) Loyalty is earned, not brought #KimMM

What is your interpretation of this statement?

_____

_____

_____

_____

56.) Depression arrives slowly. Being happy is a decision, not a given #KimMM

What is your interpretation of this statement?

_____

_____

_____

_____

57.) It's such a relief to give birth to your dreams and visions after much travail #KimMM

What is your interpretation of this statement?

_____

_____

_____

_____

58.) Don't prematurely release or hint to your next move until it's in motion #KimMM

What is your interpretation of this statement?

_____

_____

_____

_____

59.) **Having many years of experience in something means that you know better, not that you know it all #KimMM**

What is your interpretation of this statement?

_____

_____

_____

_____

60.) **Being at a place too long can give you a false since of entitlement. All the rules still apply regardless of years of service #KimMM**

What is your interpretation of this statement?

_____

_____

_____

_____

61.) **When feedback is given, be open minded and don't always try to defend your position #KimMM**

What is your interpretation of this statement?

_____

_____

_____

_____

62.) **When someone shows you your error, don't give excuses, just gracefully thank them #KimMM**

What is your interpretation of this statement?

_____

_____

_____

_____

63.) Don't enter into places with a mentality that you should be front & center because of your status. Remember you can see better from the back #KimMM

What is your interpretation of this statement?

_____

_____

_____

_____

64.) If you are resistant to change, then you are NOT prepared to go to the next level #KimMM

What is your interpretation of this statement?

_____

_____

_____

_____

65.) **If you are highly intelligent, you want people to see you as a value, NOT a threat #KimMM**

What is your interpretation of this statement?

_____

_____

_____

_____

66.) **If a person just won't listen to sound instructions from one who has experience, then let TIME teach them #KimMM**

What is your interpretation of this statement?

_____

_____

_____

_____

67.) **Volunteering your time to worthy causes keeps life in perspective. Always find something worthy to pore into #KimMM**

What is your interpretation of this statement?

_____

_____

_____

_____

68.) **When time withers away and we age, you now understand why good health outweighs riches #KimMM**

What is your interpretation of this statement?

_____

_____

_____

_____

69.) God will give you strength and strategy when blindsided by life events #KimMM

What is your interpretation of this statement?

_____

_____

_____

_____

70.) It's not because you don't have the skill to be on TOP, it's because you don't want the responsibility or headache that comes with it #KimMM

What is your interpretation of this statement?

_____

_____

_____

_____

71.) The difference between me and you is that I stayed under leadership and completed the boot camp. You prematurely started your own #KimMM

What is your interpretation of this statement?

_____

_____

_____

_____

72.) Yes, we started on the same road together, but onlookers on the sidelines lead you off track. Don't hate because your partner received a reward for staying true to the route #KimMM

What is your interpretation of this statement?

_____

_____

_____

_____

73.) Don't be so hard on your brain. Do yourself a favor and take a brain break, rest your mind, and enjoy the fruits of your labor #KimMM

What is your interpretation of this statement?

_____

_____

_____

_____

74.) It is very rare for a woman to embody strength immediately after delivery, but joy comes from knowing that the heaviness has been released #KimMM

What is your interpretation of this statement?

_____

_____

_____

_____

75.) Don't go too fast in life. Run with patience. Everyone is NOT against you advancing. Somebody wants to see you promoted, but only in due time. Stay the course #KimMM

What is your interpretation of this statement?

_____

_____

_____

_____

76.) Disagreements don't have to turn into nasty arguments; it's a time to stand up and a time to stand down #KimMM

What is your interpretation of this statement?

_____

_____

_____

_____

77.) When the storms of life are raging, be silent and still and know that God has the authority to protect you from being swept away #KimMM

What is your interpretation of this statement?

_____

_____

_____

_____

78.) Debating on touchy issues gives you enlightenment on your opponent's views #KimMM

What is your interpretation of this statement?

_____

_____

_____

_____

79.) Be cognitive when your season has ended. Take pleasure in watching from the bleachers. Cheering on others should bring you joy #KimMM

What is your interpretation of this statement?

_____

_____

_____

_____

80.) Impulsive behavior can stem from bottled stress. Recognize your pressure points through prayer #KimMM

What is your interpretation of this statement?

_____

_____

_____

_____

81.) It's imperative that we display rational conduct when being criticized #KimMM

What is your interpretation of this statement?

_____

_____

_____

_____

82.) Don't quit during recovery. Failure is one of the steps in rehabilitation. Go back at it with a champion attitude #KimMM

What is your interpretation of this statement?

_____

_____

_____

_____

83.) Those called into the ministry must demonstrate temperament regardless of the political impact #KimMM

What is your interpretation of this statement?

_____

_____

_____

_____

84.) Be careful when jumping to conclusions without details. Assumptions are the root of confusion #KimMM

What is your interpretation of this statement?

_____

_____

_____

_____

85.) Being great in the midst of snakes and scorpions is a sign you have conquered fear through faith #KimMM

What is your interpretation of this statement?

_____

_____

_____

_____

86.) Breaking a family curse starts by denouncing family secrets #KimMM

What is your interpretation of this statement?

_____

_____

_____

_____

87.) **America the beautiful, without landmarks and boundaries, are at risk of becoming a lawless nation #KimMM**

What is your interpretation of this statement?

_____

_____

_____

_____

88.) **Social media changed our methods of communicating and networking and forced us to integrate without amending the Constitution #KimMM**

What is your interpretation of this statement?

_____

_____

_____

_____

89.) Follow strict instructions by those who have authority over you. This gives them more reasons that you can be trusted for promotion #KimMM

What is your interpretation of this statement?

_____

_____

_____

_____

90.) After a chaotic day, you are very grateful for solitude. Don't rob yourself of private time #KimMM

What is your interpretation of this statement?

_____

_____

_____

_____

91.) Your heart is your internal alarm. When things just don't feel right, stop, and evaluate, and then heed the signal #KimMM

What is your interpretation of this statement?

_____

_____

_____

_____

92.) Do not be an enabler to a couch surfer. Trouble the waters. Life is no bed of ease #KimMM

What is your interpretation of this statement?

_____

_____

_____

_____

93.) Do the upcoming generations a favor; stop raising kids to think they must win all the time. You are simply raising a sore loser #KimMM

What is your interpretation of this statement?

_____

_____

_____

_____

94.) If righteousness is removed from the earth and evil is allowed to rule, the wrath of God is surely near #KimMM

What is your interpretation of this statement?

_____

_____

_____

_____

95.) Social media redefined friendship. No formal introduction needed, just a click #KimMM

What is your interpretation of this statement?

_____

_____

_____

_____

96.) We are in a season of racial insensitivity. It's imperative to describe people by hair color #KimMM

What is your interpretation of this statement?

_____

_____

_____

_____

97.) Some items of discussion may require you biting your tongue so hard that blood may be a result, but you still have dignity #KimMM

What is your interpretation of this statement?

_____

_____

_____

_____

98.) Without some type of faith and belief, you become open for garbage and rhetoric #KimMM

What is your interpretation of this statement?

_____

_____

_____

_____

99.) Examine your thoughts daily, minus yesterday's views #KimMM

What is your interpretation of this statement?

_____

_____

_____

_____

100.) Overnight sensations never imagined swift result. Always position yourself for greatness #KimMM

What is your interpretation of this statement?

_____

_____

_____

_____

Conclusion

The good news is exalted (Isaiah 52:7 (NIV). How beautiful on the mountains are the feet of those who bring good news, who proclaim peace, who bring good tidings, who proclaim salvation, who say to Zion "Your God Reigns".

Now, my dear fellow citizens of the universe, with my permission carry these phrases and tweetable moments in your arsenal and declare and share them when most needed. I hope that each quote will ultimately stimulate your mind, soul, and spirit.

#KimMM

"Now GO and tweet!"   - Kim Milton-Mackey

About the Author

Kim Milton-Mackey is a community outreach advocate and professional administrator. Kim is married to Dexter Mackey, Jr. Together they have a blended family with (7) girls and (14) grandchildren.

She has over 25 years of professional experience in advocating for social change and fighting for great causes that affect disadvantaged and underprivileged individuals. Her passion is building neighborhood campaign events that positively affect local at-risk communities. Kim is a public speaker and licensed in ministry; her focus is enhancing the lives of others through service, self-esteem, and team building.

Mrs. Milton-Mackey's mission is to strengthen existing organizations and develop millennial leaders. She serves in various political and religious settings and is experienced in dealing with a diverse population. Kim readily provides empowerment tools to the community and is known for addressing local and regional issues such as education, health care, justice, and non-violent problems. Her passion is connecting community and kingdom causes. Mrs. Milton-Mackey is employed in the Judicial System. She has a degree in business administration and is the founder of the Ingham County Cultural Diversity Employee Program.

Kim is well known for being a strategic thinker, able to inspire others to act, willing to take risks, self-motivated, and has a deep desire to work for racial and economic justice in our society. She is gifted in wisdom and is recognized for being a positive enforcement in the social media world.

Kim is the President of her own event administration and management company: Events in Excellence Promotions & Productions, LLC. The company provides marketing and management services for events and professional artists. She is highly respected and travels to various states planning events, coaching and mentoring clients.

Mrs. Milton-Mackey is the Executive Director of the non-profit organization DVM, Dreams & Visions Manifested, and Young Men of Stature. The program has assisted hundreds of young males to become great men of stature. This organization has helped plan and implement community projects and activities that have served thousands of individuals. Her organization has received support from various non-profit and religious organizations, as well as local and state government.

Kim Milton-Mackey takes pleasure in being a trailblazing author. She lives a life of inspiration, and has the compassion and skillset to motivate others. It is her desire to bring good news while empowering and leading people to a more "Excellent Way".

Kim Milton-Mackey

Event Logistics Specialist
Events in Excellence Promotions & Productions, LLC

www.events1excellence.com

"We can plan, manage and administrate in pure excellence"

Executive Director
Dreams & Visions Manifested Non-Profit Organization

www.dreamsandvisionsmanifested.com

"Connecting Community and Kingdom Affairs"

For booking or for more information on Kim, please visit either of the above websites.

61876436R00034

Made in the USA
Charleston, SC
27 September 2016